In the Know

INFLUENCERS AND TRENDS

SPORTS and FITNESS

Virginia Loh-Hagan

45TH PARALLEL PRESS

Published in the United States of America by Cherry Lake Publishing Group
Ann Arbor, Michigan
www.cherrylakepublishing.com

Reading Adviser: Marla Conn, MS, Ed., Literacy specialist, Read-Ability, Inc.
Book Designer: Felicia Macheske

Photo Credits: © Twinsterphoto/Shutterstock, cover; © Apostrophe/Shutterstock, cover; © Africa Studio/ Shutterstock, 1; © Geobor/Shutterstock, 4; © Tatiana Popova/Shutterstock, 6; © Master1305/Shutterstock, 7; © Featureflash/Dreamstime, 8; © oneinchpunch/Shutterstock, 10; © Doug James/Shutterstock, 12; © Amith Nag/Shutterstock, 14; © Tomasz Trojanowski/Shutterstock, 15; © schankz/Shutterstock, 16; © Ryan Fletcher/ Shutterstock, 18; © { QUEEN YUNA }/Flickr, 20; © gmn/Shutterstock, 22; © Flamingo Images/Shutterstock, 23; © MediaPunch Inc/Alamy Stock Photo, 24; © tomifj94/Shutterstock, 26; © National Archives Catalog/ARC ID 6802718, 28; © Zhukovsky/Dreamstime, 31

45th Parallel Press is an imprint of Cherry Lake Publishing Group.

Library of Congress Cataloging-in-Publication Data

Names: Loh-Hagan, Virginia, author.
Title: Sports and fitness / by Virginia Loh-Hagan.
Description: Ann Arbor, Michigan : Cherry Lake Publishing, 2021. | Series: In the know: Influencers and trends | Includes index. | Summary: "We're spilling the tea on the latest trends. Curious about the lives of influencers? Want to know more about extreme sports or athletes as activists? Read more to be in the know. This high-interest series is written at a low readability to aid struggling readers. Each book includes educational sidebars, throwback biographies of "OG" influencers, fast facts, and social media challenges, as well as a table of contents, glossary of keywords, index, and author biography"— Provided by publisher.
Identifiers: LCCN 2020032473 (print) | LCCN 2020032474 (ebook) | ISBN 9781534180352 (Hardcover) | ISBN 9781534182066 (Paperback) | ISBN 9781534181366 (PDF) | ISBN 9781534183070 (eBook)
Subjects: LCSH: Sports—Juvenile literature. | Physical fitness—Juvenile literature.
Classification: LCC GV705.4 .L639 2021 (print) | LCC GV705.4 (ebook) | DDC 613.7/11—dc23
LC record available at https://lccn.loc.gov/2020032473
LC ebook record available at https://lccn.loc.gov/2020032474

Cherry Lake Publishing Group would like to acknowledge the work of the Partnership for 21st Century Learning, a Network of Battelle for Kids. Please visit *http://www.battelleforkids.org/networks/p21* for more information.

Printed in the United States of America
Corporate Graphics

Dr. Virginia Loh-Hagan is an author, university professor, and former classroom teacher. June Saito was her student at San Diego State University. This book is dedicated to him. Loh-Hagan lives in San Diego with her very tall husband and very naughty dogs.

Many people follow sports and fitness influencers for workout tips. This especially became popular during the COVID-19 pandemic.

Introduction

What's **trending**? What's in? What's not? Trends are popular fads. They're widely talked about. They **dominate** the internet. Dominate means to rule over.

Influencers are people who set trends. They post a lot on **social media**. Social media are online communication platforms used to share information. Influencers post photos and videos. They post blogs and stories. They inspire a **following**. Following refers to fans. Fans make trends come to life. They spread trends. They make trends popular.

Some trends stick. Some trends don't. This book explores trends in sports and fitness.

There are many types of sports. There are team sports. There are extreme sports. There are **esports**. Esports are video game competitions. Sports include baseball, skiing, and much more. Fitness includes working out. It includes weight training. It includes stretching. Both sports and fitness are about skills. They're about physical activities. They're about moving the body.

Many people are involved in the sports and fitness communities. There are players. There are coaches. There are trainers. There are fans. Fans make stars out of sports and fitness heroes. They follow them on social media. They go to games.

Historians believe that wrestling and boxing may have been the first sports.

In 2020, Dude Perfect hosted live roller-chair hockey games online.

CHAPTER

1

Trick Shots

Shooting balls into hoops wins points. But it's not enough for social media fans. Trick shots add some fun. They add more skill. They add a unique spin. They make sports more special.

People spin balls on their fingers. They flip the balls. They mix and match sports gear. They use random household items. Things are tossed into containers. The shots seem impossible. They require some skill.

Dude Perfect is one of the top YouTube channels. It's a sports entertainment channel. It's owned by 5 guys. The guys went to college together. Their most popular videos are trick shots. They add in upbeat music.

They set several world records. For example, they did the highest basketball shot. (However, this record was broken by Australian YouTube stars How Ridiculous in 2016.) They stood on top of a building. They were 533 feet (162 meters) above a hoop. They made the shot.

They've become very successful. They've made video games. They've written books. They have their own canned beans. They have their own TV show. They have a movie.

They were one of the first to make trick shots popular. They inspired others. For example, June Saito is a skateboarder. He also does trick shot videos. He throws red cups. He throws cups backward without looking. They land in a container or perfectly stacked on top of each other. He said, "Everyone seems to believe that I rigged the trick shots somehow, but everything is 100 percent real."

◄ There are many trick shot videos on the internet.

Stunts can cause injuries. Travis Pastrana has broken over 60 bones. He's had 25 head injuries.

CHAPTER

2

Stunts

Stunts are unusual or difficult performances. They require skill. They can be risky. There are all types of stunts. There are no rules.

In 2020, people stayed at home to slow the spread of COVID-19. Stunt workers do stunts for movies and TV. A group of stunt workers made a video. They each did fighting stunts at their own homes. They edited the videos together. They made one fight scene. The video went **viral**. Viral means spread quickly. The video has over 15 million views on Twitter.

Travis Pastrana is a professional stuntman. He has over 3.9 million Instagram followers. He jumped over 52 cars. He jumped over 16 buses. He does double backflips on his bike.

BE A LITTLE EXTRA

SOCIAL MEDIA CHALLENGE

Produce a trick shot video on TikTok. Use only things you can find in your house.

Be safe. Make sure you don't hurt yourself or others. Don't throw sharp things. Don't throw things at people.

Practice tricks around the house. Start with easy trick shots. Toss a tea bag into a large cup. Toss bread into a toaster.

Choose your favorite trick shot activity. Do this after you try different things.

Practice more. Change the distance. Start close. Keep moving farther apart.

Make the shots a little harder. Add flips. Throw backward.

Decide if you want to talk or not. Decide if you want to add music.

Capture everything. Choose what you want to share. Edit your video clips. Share it with your friends.

Fabio Wibmer is a stunt **cyclist**. Cyclists ride bikes. Wibmer has about 6 million followers on social media. He's active on YouTube and Instagram. He uploads videos of his failures, stunts, and pranks. His stunt videos have gotten over 500 million views. He rode his bike downstairs. He balanced his bike on top of a high dam. He used his back wheel to kick a basketball into a hoop.

Melanie Hunt is a professional **parkour athlete**. Parkour combines running, gymnastics, martial arts, and breakdancing. Athletes are people trained in sports and fitness. A parkour athlete moves through obstacles. Hunt did parkour stunts around New York City, New York. She wore fancy clothes. This was for an art project.

In 2020, Wibmer turned his house into a bike park. He rode his bike around his house.

Some people will wear bathing suits while doing snow sports.

CHAPTER 3

Taking Extreme to the Extreme

Extreme sports are action sports. They have high speeds. They have high risk.

Rock climbing is already extreme. Even more extreme, is naked rock climbing. Naked rock climbers don't wear clothes. They feel closer to nature. Naked rock climbing increases the difficulty level. Being naked means climbers don't have any protection or safety gear. Halsey is a singer. She has over 20 million Instagram followers. She posted pictures of injuries from naked rock climbing.

Roberta Mancino is a model. She does extreme sports. She's a skydiver, BASE jumper, and wingsuit flyer. She's also done 4 naked skydiving jumps. She has over 90,000 Instagram followers.

BREITLING

Wing-walking is an extremely extreme sport. It's the act of moving along the wings of a small plane during flight. Some people wing-walk from one plane to another. Sammy Mason is a **pilot**. Pilots fly planes. Mason is the youngest pilot to be part of the Red Bull Air Race. He performs in air shows. He also competes in air races. He has over 20,000 Instagram followers. He posted pictures of himself wing-walking.

There are other ways to make extreme sports extreme. Imagine **bungee** jumping over a river of crocodiles. Bungees are long bouncy ropes. Imagine diving or boarding into a volcano. All these feats are posted on Instagram.

◂ People do extreme sports because they like surviving danger.

Athleisure wear is more breathable, lighter, and water-resistant.

CHAPTER 4

Athleisure Wear

Fashion changes all the time. Fashion means clothing styles. Athleisure is trendy now. It combines the words *athlete* and **leisure**. Leisure means free time from work. Athleisure wear is a mix of workout clothes and **loungewear**. Loungewear is casual clothes. It includes pajamas. It includes T-shirts.

Athleisure has many purposes. It can be worn at the gym. It can be worn at home. It can be worn at school. It can be worn at work. It's comfortable. It's stylish. It comes in different colors. It comes in different designs.

There are many types of athleisure wear. Athleisure wear includes leggings. It includes sneakers. It includes shorts. It includes tank tops. It includes jackets.

Spilling the TEA

SPORTS AND FITNESS INFLUENCERS

Did you know...

- Richard Simmons was born in 1948. He's a fitness trainer. He's known for his lively personality. He helped people lose weight. He owned a gym. He did TV shows. He made workout videotapes. He did aerobics. His videotapes are called "Sweatin' to the Oldies." He was on a lot of radio and talk shows. He was really popular.

- Cristiano Ronaldo is a professional soccer player. He's from Portugal. He's thought to be the world's best player. He's the most popular athlete online. He has over 400 million followers across all his social media accounts. He has over 900 million interactions. He's the most followed person on Instagram. He's Instagram's highest earner. He makes more money from social media than soccer.

- Allysha Le is a skater. She has over 101,000 followers on Instagram. She started skateboarding at age 7. She competed in the X Games at age 12. She was the youngest competitor. She's "focusing on having fun."

The athleisure trend started with women wearing yoga pants. Women would wear these pants everywhere. They'd also wear them for different events without having to change. This made things easier. People wouldn't have to carry extra clothes.

Kylie Jenner is a high-earning Instagram influencer. She has close to 200 million followers. She's known for mixing athleisure with fancy clothes. She wears bike shorts with fancy tops. She wears leggings with fancy heels. She wears jumpsuits. She wears bodysuits. She wears **cropped** sweatshirts. Cropped means cut.

TikTok is dominated by dancing. So, athleisure wear is popular on TikTok. Charli D'Amelio has almost 100 million followers. She's the "queen of TikTok." She used her fame to encourage people to stay home during the 2020 pandemic.

▲ Athleisure wear is also called sportswear or fitness fashion.

Many wellness coaches post motivational messages.

CHAPTER 5

Wellness Coaches

Wellness means being in good health. It includes mental health. It includes physical health. Wellness coaches are a new trend. People want to be healthy. They seek help. They hire wellness coaches. Or they follow wellness coaches online.

Wellness coaches give people tips. They help people make healthy choices. They help people meet their lifestyle goals. They help people become their best selves. They're support partners. Many wellness coaches are influencers.

Jennifer Leigh Selter has millions of followers on Instagram. She is a fitness, nutrition, and lifestyle coach. She started as a front desk clerk at a gym. She built an online community. She encourages her followers to post their training results.

Fitness is a passion for many people. They share their journeys online. The hashtag #FitTok allows TikTok fitness influencers to show off. Fitness influencers post workouts. They post tips. They post dances. Antonie Lokhurst is an online fitness coach. He posts fun fitness challenges on TikTok. He did a push-up challenge that got almost 5 million views. He posted a video using his cats as weights.

A new trend is influencers hiring wellness coaches. Victoria Spence has over 100,000 Instagram followers. She struggled with an eating disorder. But she overcame it. She focused on getting healthy. She became a bodybuilder. Now, she's a personal trainer and fitness influencer. But like everyone, she gets stressed. She hired a wellness coach. She said, "It helps to have somebody backing you all the way."

◂ Using fitness apps became a hot trend during the pandemic in 2020.

The Brooklyn Dodgers fought to integrate baseball in the 1940s. Integrate means to include people of all ethnicities.

CHAPTER

6

Athletes as Activists

Today, athletes are more than just sports stars. They're also **activists**. Activists are people who fight for change. They fight for justice. They fight for equal rights.

Colin Kaepernick is a professional football player. He played for the San Francisco 49ers. He's also a civil rights activist. He's best known for kneeling during the national anthem. He did this during football games. He protested police brutality. He supported #BlackLivesMatter. He said, "I am not going to stand up to show pride in a flag for a country that oppresses Black people and people of color." In 2020, he started a fund. He wanted to help people protesting George Floyd's death. Floyd was killed by a police officer. His last words were, "I can't breathe."

THROWBACK OG INFLUENCER

There were influencers before social media. An original (or "OG") sports and fitness influencer was George Herman "Babe" Ruth. Ruth lived from 1895 to 1948. He was an American professional baseball player. He played during the 1920s. This was known as the Golden Age of American Sports. People traveled to watch games. They paid to root for their home teams. They listened to games on the radio. They read about games in the newspapers. Baseball was the most popular sport. And Babe Ruth was the most popular baseball player. He played for the New York Yankees. He set records. He had an exciting personality. He was confident. He was funny. He liked to do radio shows. He liked to do newspaper stories. He appeared in newspaper ads. He made money from his fame. He made more money than the U.S. president. He had a lot of fans. His fans called him "The Bambino." He's the first celebrity athlete.

LeBron James is a professional basketball player. He played for the L.A. Lakers. He has millions of Twitter followers. His Twitter handle is @KingJames. He wore a special pair of sneakers. One was black. One was white. The sneakers had "equality" written on the back.

Gabby Douglas is a gymnast. She's won 3 gold medals. She's one of the youngest winners. She's the first African American to be the Olympic all-around champion. She has over a million Instagram followers. She fights against bullying. She visits colleges. She visits high schools. She talks about being kind. She said, "I want to show people that no matter how bad it gets, you can do something about it."

▲ More famous people are using their names and star power to raise awareness.

Glossary

activists (AK-tih-vists) people who fight for political or social change

athlete (ATH-leet) a person who trains for sports or fitness

bungee (BUN-jee) a long bouncy rope

cropped (KRAHPD) cut short

cyclist (SYE-klist) a person who rides a bike

dominate (DAH-muh-nate) to rule over

esports (EE-sports) video game competitions

following (FAH-loh-ing) fans or supporters

influencers (IN-floo-uhns-urz) people who set trends by posting a lot on social media and have large followings

leisure (LEE-zhur) free time from school or work

loungewear (LOUNJ-wair) casual, comfortable clothes

parkour (PAHR-kor) an extreme sport that combines running, gymnastics, martial arts, and breakdancing that requires the athlete to move through obstacles

pilot (PYE-luht) a person who flies planes

social media (SOH-shuhl MEE-dee-uh) online communications used to share information

trending (TREND-ing) currently a popular fad online

viral (VYE-ruhl) trending or spreading very quickly

wellness (WEL-nis) being in good health

Learn More

Loh-Hagan, Virginia. *Extreme Rock Climbing*. Ann Arbor, MI: Cherry Lake Publishing, 2015.

Loh-Hagan, Virginia. *Wacky Sports*. Ann Arbor, MI: Cherry Lake Publishing, 2017.

Index